VIRGINIA

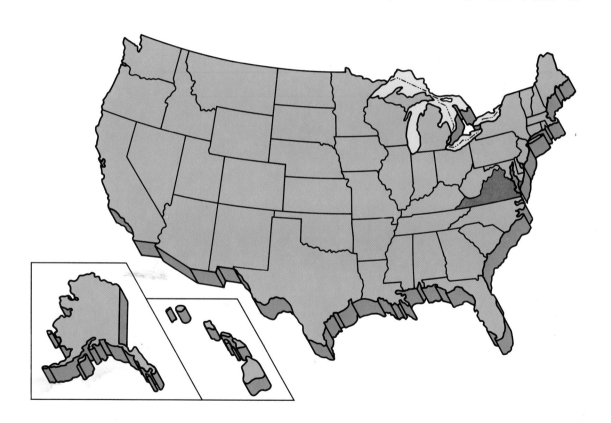

Hello U★S★A★

VIRGINIA

Karen Sirvaitis

Lerner Publications Company

LIBRARY OF CONGRESS
CATALOGING-IN-PUBLICATION DATA
Sirvaitis, Karen.
    Virginia / Karen Sirvaitis.
        p.   cm. — (Hello USA)
    Includes index.
    Summary: Introduces the geography, history, people, industries, and other highlights of Virginia.
        ISBN 0-8225-2702-2 (lib. bdg.)
    1. Virginia—Juvenile literature.
[1. Virginia.] I. Title. II. Series.
F226.3.S57   1991
975.5—dc20   90-6483
                                CIP
                                AC

Manufactured in the United States of America
1 2 3 4 5 6 7 8 9 10 99 98 97 96 95 94 93 92 91

Cover photograph courtesy of Virginia Division of Tourism.

The glossary that begins on page 68 gives definitions of words shown in **bold type** in the text.

 This book is printed on recycled paper.

CONTENTS

Queen Elizabeth I (1533–1603)

Did You Know . . . ?

☐ Virginia is named after England's Queen Elizabeth I, who never married and was known as the Virgin Queen.

☐ You can thank a Virginian, Thomas Jefferson, for the tomatoes in your salad. Before he bit into one in the 1700s, many people believed the fruit to be poisonous.

☐ Virginia's Blue Ridge Mountains got their name from their trees, which from a distance appear to be blue.

In Arlington, Virginia, 15,000 meals are served each day at the Pentagon, one of the largest office buildings in the world.

Virginians who want to help keep their state clean can "Adopt-a-Spot." Armed with brooms and trash bags, volunteers are in charge of keeping their adopted spot free of litter.

What do Presidents George Washington, Thomas Jefferson, James Madison, James Monroe, William Henry Harrison, John Tyler, Zachary Taylor, and Woodrow Wilson have in common? They were all born in Virginia. More U.S. presidents were born in Virginia than in any other state.

Jack-in-the-pulpit

A Trip Around the State

Virginia once stretched from the coast of the Atlantic Ocean far into the midwestern United States. Because nine states were eventually formed from its original boundaries, Virginia has been called the Mother of States.

9

Virginia still rests midway along the East Coast. The state's present-day boundaries meet the District of Columbia and five southern states—Maryland, West Virginia, Kentucky, Tennessee, and North Carolina. The Chesapeake Bay and the Atlantic Ocean wash against Virginia's coastline.

Virginia's landscape varies from steep mountains to shallow **marshes.** The mountains tower above western Virginia in the Appalachian Highland region. The Piedmont and the Tidewater, two other regions, occupy the rest of the state.

Wet lowlands are common near Virginia's coast.

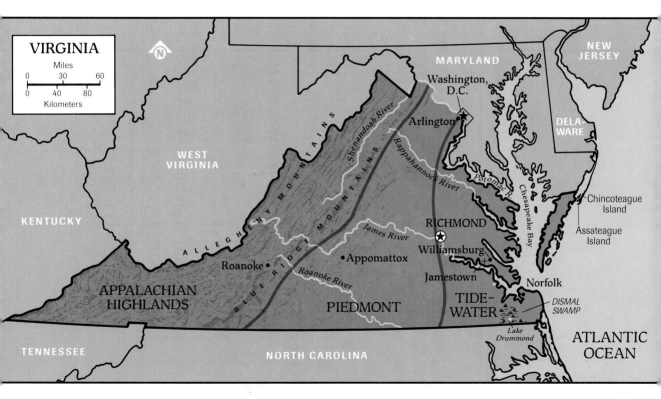

VIRGINIA

Miles
0   30   60

0   40   80
Kilometers

N

WEST
VIRGINIA

MARYLAND

NEW
JERSEY

Washington,
D.C.

Arlington

DELA-
WARE

KENTUCKY

Shenandoah River

Rappahannock River

Potomac R.

Chincoteague
Island

Assateague
Island

Chesapeake Bay

RICHMOND

James River

Williamsburg

Roanoke

• Appomattox

Jamestown

Norfolk

APPALACHIAN
HIGHLANDS

Roanoke River

PIEDMONT

TIDE-
WATER

*DISMAL
SWAMP*

TENNESSEE

NORTH CAROLINA

Lake
Drummond

ATLANTIC
OCEAN

The valleys of the Blue Ridge Mountains have rich soil that makes good farmland.

The Appalachian Highlands feature part of the oldest and second longest mountain chain in North America. Called the Appalachian Mountains, these peaks took their shape slowly, beginning millions of years ago.

The Appalachians include the Allegheny Mountains, whose high peaks kept some early Virginians from traveling farther west. Another range of the Appalachians—the Blue Ridge Mountains—lies east of the Alleghenies. All of these ranges slope downward into valleys, through which many rivers and streams flow. You may have sung songs about Shenandoah, the largest river valley in Virginia.

White-tailed deer roam freely at Chincoteague National Wildlife Refuge.

In the fall, orchard growers harvest bushels of apples.

The Piedmont begins where the Blue Ridge Mountains end. The name *Piedmont* comes from an Italian word that means "foot of the mountain." This region, with its clusters of grazing cattle and rows of apple trees, covers central Virginia from north to south.

Eastern Virginia is known as the Tidewater region (also called the Atlantic Coastal Plain). Rivers, **bays,** and **lagoons** break up the coastal land of the Tidewater and shape Virginia's ragged shoreline. Marshes (soft wetlands) are common, especially near the Chesapeake Bay, and beaches stretch along the Atlantic Ocean. A few miles inland, farmers plant crops.

Virginia's Tidewater region includes a large **peninsula** (land surrounded by water on three sides) called the Eastern Shore. The Chesapeake Bay separates this peninsula from the major portion of the state. Many islands lie off the Eastern Shore.

Several rivers—including the Shenandoah, Potomac, Rappahannock, James, and Roanoke—flow through Virginia. Large ships transport cargo on a few of the deep eastern rivers.

By damming, or blocking, Virginia's rivers, people have created many artificial lakes. But the state has only a few natural lakes. The largest of these is Lake Drummond. Its still waters lie within a large wetland called the Dismal Swamp, in southeastern Virginia. The **swamp** is overgrown with creeping vines and sprawling bald cypress trees.

Asters *(above)* **brighten a mountainside. A monarch caterpillar** *(top right)* **rests on a milkweed leaf.**

Sweet-smelling scents from flowering shrubs, such as dogwood and mountain laurel, fill Virginia's warm spring air. The state's summers are long, lasting into October. But later that month, the trees turn shades of red, yellow, and orange, marking the beginning of fall. Winters are short, especially in the east where the occasional snow melts quickly. Rainfall is heaviest along the coast.

Forests of oak, pine, hickory, and tulip trees cover more than half of Virginia. During the spring

Grazing on tall grasses, the ponies of Assateague Island pass the time.

and summer, brightly colored wildflowers highlight the lush, green valleys and the mountains.

If you venture into these mountains, you might see a black bear, a bobcat, or one of Virginia's many other animals. Along the coast, the state hosts a variety of underwater wildlife. Oysters, crabs, and other shellfish abound.

Off the Eastern Shore, bands of wild ponies roam Assateague Island. According to legend, ancestors of the ponies swam to the island from a sinking Spanish ship more than 400 years ago.

The manner of their fishing.

In the late 1500s, John White became one of the first English artists to explore Virginia. He painted pictures *(left)* of plants, animals, and people in the region. He also made maps *(facing page)* of Virginia's coastline.

Virginia's Story

Imagine Virginia hundreds of years ago, when European explorers stumbled upon the Americas and called them the "New World." At that time—in the late 1400s—three major Native American (Indian) groups made their home in the area. They were the Cherokee, the Susquehanna, and the Algonquians.

The Algonquians lived in the Tidewater region. They knew the land well and could farm, hunt, and fish with ease. The Algonquians sometimes united their villages and followed one leader, or chief. By 1580 a chief named Powhatan had ruled a group that was 200 villages strong.

At the same time, across the Atlantic Ocean in the British Isles, a few leaders were planning a journey. They wanted to send some English people to North America to set up a British **colony**. The British leaders believed the new colony would be rich with gold.

In 1587 the first shiploads of English people reached the eastern coast of the continent. They claimed a large part of the shore and much of the area between the Atlantic and Pacific oceans. They named this land Virginia.

Until the very early 1600s, the settlers who came to the British colony of Virginia either died, mysteriously disappeared, or returned to Great Britain. But the 104 colonists who came in the spring of 1607 were more successful. They were able to establish the first British settlement to survive in the New World.

These colonists arrived by ship at the mouth of what is now called the James River. They anchored in Powhatan's territory.

The newcomers unloaded their ships and named their new home Jamestown, after James I, king of Great Britain. Although many were educated, most of the residents of Jamestown had never farmed the land or built a home. They knew little about living in the wilderness.

The British colonists arrived at the James River aboard three ships—the *Godspeed,* the *Susan Constant,* and the *Discovery*—on May 13, 1607.

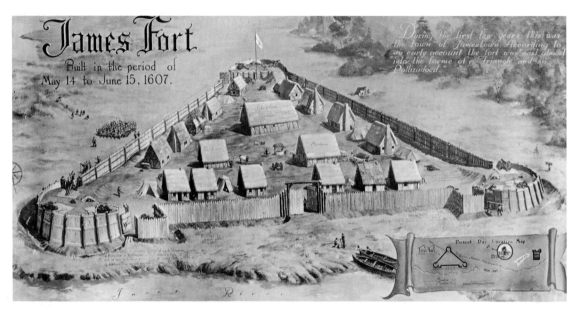

The new settlers began building James Fort on May 14, 1607, the day after they landed.

One man, Captain John Smith, taught the colonists to plant crops, to fish, and to build a fort to protect themselves against possible dangers. He knew their survival would be difficult, so he enforced a strict law—those who did not work did not eat. Smith also made friends with Chief Powhatan and traded kettles, jewelry, and other items to the Algonquians for much needed food.

Chief Powhatan suspected the strangers came to do more than trade. He feared the colonists wanted to take over the land where the Algonquians lived. The two groups often fought each other.

In 1609 Captain Smith was burned badly in a gunpowder explosion, and he returned to Britain. The following winter is known as the "starving time" because the settlers did not have enough food. Suffering from disease and hunger, they ate almost anything—even rats and snakes. Nearly all the colonists died. Just as the few survivors were ready to go home, a shipload of people and food arrived from Britain.

Before he became a chief, Powhatan was known as Wahunsenacawh.

23

A Dutch slave ship anchored off Virginia's coast in 1619. The hungry sailors traded 20 of their captives to the colonists for food and fresh water. These first blacks in Virginia were indentured servants—people who were forced to work for other people for several years before earning their freedom. Within 50 years, however, blacks would become slaves.

The first general assembly in America met at Jamestown in 1619. This group spoke for, or represented, the colonists of Virginia on matters such as taxes.

Fighting between the Indians and the colonists continued. They agreed to live peacefully beside each other only after Powhatan's daughter, Pocahontas, married a colonist named John Rolfe in 1614.

Pocahontas

One of the first female heroes recorded in the history of the Virginia colony was a young Indian, a daughter of Chief Powhatan. Her name was Pocahontas, which meant "playful child" in an Algonquian language.

Pocahontas was about 12 years old in 1607 when the British landed in Virginia. Shortly after the newcomers arrived, the Algonquians captured the settlers' captain, John Smith. The Indians probably wanted to learn more about Smith or even to adopt him. But according to Smith's version of the story, the Indians planned to kill him.

One day, after a big feast, Powhatan ordered his men to bind Smith's hands. A few Indians closed in on Smith with raised clubs. But before the men could strike, Pocahontas lunged between Smith and the weapons. Chief Powhatan ordered that Smith be released.

The relieved captain thought Pocahontas had saved his life. If she did prevent his death, Pocahontas also saved the colonists who depended upon Smith for their survival.

Pocahontas and Smith became good friends. Smith taught her to speak English, and she helped Smith learn Algonquian.

In 1614, several years after the Indians captured Smith, Pocahontas married colonist John Rolfe. Because of the marriage, the Indians and the settlers were friendlier toward each other. The Algonquians and the British did not fight again until after Powhatan's death in 1618.

Pocahontas died at about the age of 22. She and Rolfe were visiting Great Britain when she caught a disease called smallpox. Her husband and their young son, Thomas, remained in Britain, where the boy went to school. Thomas later returned to Virginia and raised a family. Some Virginians claim to be descendants of the heroine's family.

27

Tobacco was the first money-making crop grown by the colonists.

The colonists soon needed something valuable to send to Britain in exchange for more clothing and other necessities. They had not unearthed any gold, as they had originally thought they might. But John Rolfe discovered something else well worth trading.

Rolfe found some tobacco seeds while shipwrecked in the West Indies. He planted the seeds once he arrived in Virginia. Tobacco was easy to grow in Virginia's soil and climate. Planters sent samples of their product to Britain, and smokers there wanted more.

Before long, the colonists were growing the plant almost everywhere—even between the cracks in the streets! Some tobacco farmers became rich, and they built **plantations** (large farms) on what had been the Indians' homeland.

Chief Powhatan died in 1618. Future Algonquian chiefs waged two major wars to gain back their territory from the colonists. The last attempt to get rid of the British ended in

In 1676 Nathaniel Bacon *(right)* led a rebellion against Virginia's governor William Berkeley *(left)*. Bacon wanted fewer trade laws and protection from Indians. The rebels burned down the Governor's Palace in Jamestown.

1644. Gradually, the farmers forced the Native Americans farther and farther west.

During the 1600s and 1700s, both the British and the French explored parts of North America and claimed some of the same land. In 1754 the two groups began fighting a war (called the French and Indian War) to settle these claims. Many Indians sided with the French, but the French lost the war in 1763. At least one officer from Virginia fought bravely for the British. His name was George Washington.

Patrick Henry urged members of the Second Virginia Convention to gather an army for the upcoming revolution against Britain. His speech ended with the famous words "Give me liberty or give me death!"

George Washington was 40 years old when his first portrait was painted in 1772.

To help pay the costs of the French and Indian War, Britain charged the colonists taxes on everyday items such as sugar and tea. The colonists were angry. A small group of Virginians gathered to talk about the new British laws. Members of the group included Patrick Henry, Thomas Jefferson, and George Washington.

In 1774 a few of these people met with leaders from the other colonies at the First Continental Congress in Philadelphia. The Congress decided that unless Britain stopped charging unreasonable taxes, the colonists would not buy British goods.

Britain, however, continued to tax tea. Tension mounted and the first gunshot of the American Revolution (the war between Britain and the 13 colonies) was fired in Massachusetts in 1775. George Washington now fought against the British as commander-in-chief of the colonial forces.

Thomas Jefferson wrote the Declaration of Independence and became the third president of the United States. He died on July 4, 1826, exactly 50 years after the signing of the Declaration.

On May 15, 1776, Virginians declared their colony independent of British rule. Soon afterward, on July 4, 1776, the Continental Congress approved Thomas Jefferson's Declaration of Independence, which stated that all 13 colonies were breaking ties with Britain.

Most of the fighting in the Revolution took place in other colonies, but the last major battle ended at Yorktown, Virginia, in 1781. Here, with the help of the French army and navy (the British and French were still enemies), colonial forces defeated British troops. The war officially ended in 1783, when both sides signed a peace agreement.

The British surrendered to colonial forces at Yorktown, Virginia, in 1781.

George Washington worked with members of the Continental Congress to write a **constitution**. After the people of a colony accepted the laws in the U.S. Constitution, that colony became a member of the Union—that is, the United States of America.

Virginia became the tenth state on June 25, 1788. One year later, the people of the Union elected George Washington as the first president of the United States.

As the young nation grew during the 1800s, the Northern states built many factories, and the Southern states continued to farm. The lifestyles of Northerners and Southerners became very different. They disagreed on many issues, including the South's wide use of

Most slaves worked long, hard days farming their master's land.

slaves (people who are owned by other people).

By 1861 several Southern states had withdrawn from the Union to form the Confederate States of America, a separate country that allowed slavery. Abraham Lincoln, who was then the U.S. president, sent troops into the South. The Civil War between the Northern and Southern states had begun.

Virginians did not want to go to war. They had waited until the North declared war before joining the Confederate, or Southern, army. Richmond, Virginia, became the capital of the Confederate States.

35

Although he was against slavery, Robert E. Lee remained loyal to his home state during the Civil War.

Most Virginians who lived in the state's northwestern mountains still supported the North. In 1863 this part of Virginia became a separate state called West Virginia.

Robert E. Lee, a Virginian, led the Confederates to many victories during the Civil War. But in 1865, a Union army general, Ulysses S. Grant, forced General Lee and his troops to surrender at Appomattox, Virginia. President Lincoln had already called for all the slaves in the Confederate States to be freed.

The war was over, but for Virginians more hardship lay ahead. More Civil War battles had been fought in Virginia than in any other state. Cities and plantations lay in ruins.

Confederate soldiers surrendered Richmond to the Union army only after destroying their valuables by setting the city on fire.

During a period known as **Reconstruction,** the U.S. government helped reconstruct, or rebuild, the war-torn South. Slowly, Virginia recovered. Virginians approved a new state constitution and in 1870 rejoined the United States.

Virginia's people began to rely not only on farming but also on manufacturing. Factories were built, and their owners hired workers to make cloth, cigarettes, and ships. These new jobs encouraged people to stay in the state.

In 1912 a Virginian, Woodrow Wilson, was elected president. During Wilson's term, World War I broke out in Europe. The U.S. military trained soldiers and pilots at camps set up in Virginia. After the war, the U.S. government built the Norfolk Naval Base, the largest naval base in the country. In the early 1940s, Virginia again became a military base for U.S. soldiers serving in World War II.

After the war, black people united to work for their **civil rights,** or personal freedoms. Black people had been segregated (separated or kept apart) from white people. Blacks and whites were not allowed, for example, to attend the same schools. In 1954, however, the U.S. Supreme Court ruled that students—whether black or white— must share classrooms.

One segregation law required that black passengers ride only at the back of buses and streetcars (facing page).

Several of Virginia's schools closed because some people still wanted to keep students segregated. In 1959 the court ordered the state to follow the law, and all but one school system reopened that year. Since then, schools in Virginia have been integrated—that is, blacks and whites learn together in the same classrooms.

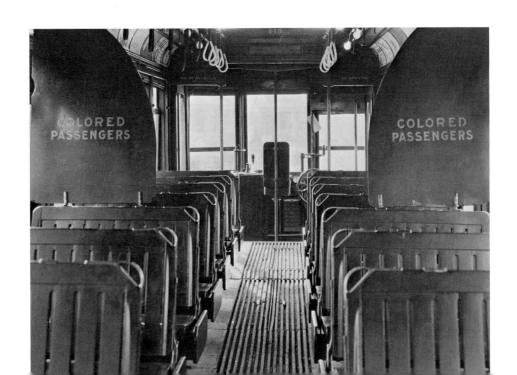

1492

1607

Europeans discover the New World

Colonists arrive in Virginia and build Jamestown

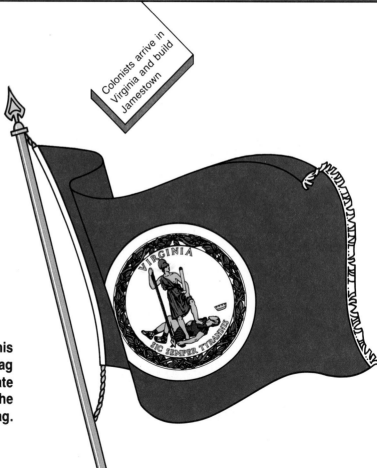

Virginia has used this design for its state flag since 1861. The state seal appears in the center of the flag.

Virginians begin fighting in the French and Indian War (1754-1763)

American Revolutionary War (1775-1783) begins

Thomas Jefferson writes the Declaration of Independence

Virginia becomes the 10th state to join the Union

The Civil War (1861-1865) begins, and Virginia becomes a major battleground

U.S. Supreme Court rules against segregation

Virginians choose the nation's first elected black governor

Virginians uphold many laws based on the U.S. Constitution, which George Washington helped write more than 200 years ago. One of these laws gives people the right to vote. In 1989, using this right, Virginians elected Douglas Wilder to serve as **governor** of their state. Wilder is the first elected black governor in the country.

This warship was built by Newport News Shipbuilding Company in Newport News, Virginia. Shipbuilders in Virginia make both military and commercial ships.

Living and Working in Virginia

Times have changed since 1607, when the colonists first settled in Virginia. More than six million people now live in the state. As in the 1600s, some people farm tobacco fields or fish the Chesapeake Bay. Others, however, work in computerized textile (cloth) mills or with high-tech military equipment.

The Pentagon gets its name from its shape. The building has five sides and five corners.

About one-third of Virginia's people live in rural areas, and many of them are farmers. Most Virginians live and work in or near the cities of Norfolk, Arlington, Roanoke, and Richmond—the capital.

The cities in northeastern Virginia are home to thousands of people who commute to work in neighboring Washington, D.C. A huge office building called the Pentagon stands in Arlington, a city near the nation's capital. Twenty-three thousand people work in the Pentagon for the U.S. Department of Defense. Farther south, in Norfolk, the U.S. government operates the Norfolk Naval Base.

Most of the state's population are white people whose ancestors came from Great Britain or Germany. Black people make up almost 20 percent of the population. Native Americans number slightly over 9,000—less than 1 percent of Virginia's population. Most of Virginia's recent **immigrants** (newcomers) are of Hispanic or Southeast-Asian origin.

Virginians built the country's first free, or public, school in 1634. They called it Syms Free School. Many children could not attend Syms, however, because they lived too far away. Most Virginians could get an education after the

The number of Southeast Asians in Virginia is increasing.

Civil War, when the state started paying for public education. Now, more than one million children attend Virginia's public schools.

45

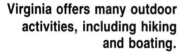
Virginia offers many outdoor
activities, including hiking
and boating.

During the summer, Virginians
sunbathe and water-ski at the
Chesapeake Bay and the Atlantic
Ocean. Sailboats, motorboats, and
yachts crowd the waters and dock

along the shores of the bay. People also hike on the trails in the
Appalachians—a place to get plenty of exercise while admiring the
scenery.

Costumed in bright riding gear, fox hunters and their dogs head for the woods.

Fox hunting, a tradition the colonists carried over from Britain, is still a familiar sport in northern Virginia. Groups of riders on horseback, surrounded by dozens of hunting dogs, often spend hours tracking foxes on the grounds of old plantations.

The people who live in Virginia's Appalachian Highlands follow customs that have been passed down from generation to generation. Fiddlers, or violinists, play lively, toe-tapping music at local square dances. Some of the craftspeople make musical instruments called dulcimers. These stringed instruments and other artworks are displayed each August at the Highlands Arts and Crafts Festival in Abingdon.

Virginians are proud of their rich past. Part of Williamsburg, the state's capital from 1699 to 1780, has been rebuilt to look the way it did in colonial days. Women who work in the historic town wear bonnets and long, full skirts. Men dress in ruffled shirts, knee breeches, and powdered wigs.

The Museum of the Confederacy displays uniforms, weapons, and documents from the Civil War. The Mariners' Museum features the history of ships and shipping in the United States. And the Barter Theatre, situated in the mountains, presents many well-known plays. It got its name in the 1930s, when people bartered—or traded—pigs, chickens, flowers, and other goods for admission.

The Fife and Drum Corps of Williamsburg, Virginia, brings colonial history to life. In the past, fife players and drummers accompanied military units.

During the Civil War, this mansion was the home of Confederate president Jefferson Davis. The building is known as the White House of the Confederacy and is part of the Museum of the Confederacy in Richmond.

Tobacco, the crop that grew well for Virginia's colonists, is still the state's leading harvest. Only a small number of farmers actually grow the plant, but more Virginians work in tobacco processing than in any other industry. Most farmers sell milk, beef, chickens, turkeys, and hogs. Virginia is famous for its Smithfield hams, which are cut from hogs that were fed mostly peanuts.

51

Coal is transported from the Appalachian Highlands in railroad cars.

Virginia's most important mineral is coal, most of which is dug from deep underground. When burned, coal releases energy. Many power plants across the United States use this form of energy to produce electricity. Virginia is a leading coal-producing state.

Many Virginians work in factories that make chemicals, ships, clothing, or tobacco products—mainly cigarettes. Some people fish for a living. They bring in oysters, crabs, clams, and scallops from the Chesapeake Bay. At nearby factories, these shellfish are packaged to be sold.

A worker examines the propeller of a commercial ship that needs repair.

Virginia's products are shipped from several major port cities in the state. Large freighters anchor easily in the deep harbors of the Chesapeake Bay. The harbors in the Norfolk area export more weight in goods than any other port in the United States.

In the past, Virginians had to drive through neighboring Maryland or take a ferryboat across the Bay to reach the Eastern Shore. But in 1964, the state completed the Chesapeake Bay Bridge-Tunnel. The continuous bridge-tunnel is 17 miles long. Now it's possible to drive across the bay between Norfolk and the peninsula.

From a skipjack, watermen dredge oysters from the floor of the Chesapeake Bay.

Protecting the Environment

On the Chesapeake Bay, Virginians harvest oysters and load them onto sailing vessels called skipjacks. But the skipjacks are not as full of shellfish as they were 20 years ago. Boaters still cruise the bay in colorful sailboats, but some swimmers have chosen to go elsewhere. Life in and around the bay is changing because parts of the bay's ecosystem are changing.

An ecosystem can be thought of as a household. Just as a household has both living and nonliving things, an ecosystem has plants and animals (living things) and soil, air, and water (nonliving things). Each living thing needs nutrients (nourishment needed for health) and depends on other members in its ecosystem for these nutrients.

Bald eagles are part of the Chesapeake Bay's ecosystem.

Some of the fertilizers used on fields in the hills of western Virginia eventually drain into the bay.

Nutrients occur naturally in the bay's water. But they also have been entering the water from sources outside the bay. For example, to make crops and lawns grow better, people apply fertilizers. Fertilizers contain nutrients in the form of nitrogen and phosphorous. Eventually, rain washes some of the fertilizer into the bay or into rivers that drain into the bay. This process is called **nutrient runoff.**

Another source that brings nutrients into the Chesapeake Bay is wastewater. Wastewater is the water that carries sewage from homes, businesses, and industries to sewage treatment plants. Wastewater contains many nutrients that come from the sewage it carries. When wastewater reaches the treatment plants, it is filtered, cleansed, and then released into rivers or the bay. Treating wastewater, however, does not remove any of its nutrients.

Forty-eight rivers, some with tributaries as far north as New York, flow into the bay. These waterways carry both nutrient runoff and treated wastewater from six states and 15 million people. The great number of nutrients entering the Chesapeake Bay has changed the bay's ecosystem. Some of its members are multiplying rapidly, while others are dying.

Factories, as well as households and businesses, add to the pollution in the bay.

A Changing Ecosystem

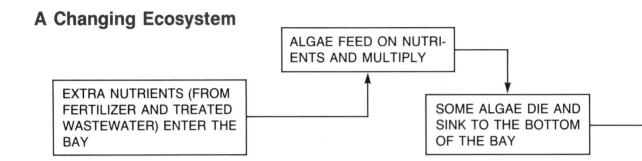

EXTRA NUTRIENTS (FROM FERTILIZER AND TREATED WASTEWATER) ENTER THE BAY

ALGAE FEED ON NUTRIENTS AND MULTIPLY

SOME ALGAE DIE AND SINK TO THE BOTTOM OF THE BAY

For instance, algae, small rootless plants that live just under the water's surface, feed on the many nutrients in the bay and grow very thick. A certain amount of algae is good. They are a source of food for fish. But the algae in the bay are so thick that the fish do not eat all of them. Eventually, the plants that do not get eaten die and sink to the bottom of the bay.

Dead plants are food for bacteria (tiny, one-celled organisms). The bacteria at the bottom of the bay multiply easily because of all the dead plants there. All these bacteria use a lot of oxygen, another nutrient needed by living things.

The bottom of the Chesapeake does not have enough oxygen for both the bacteria and all the bay's underwater wildlife. When bacteria thrive in an area of the bay, many of the fish and oysters, which cannot get enough oxygen, either die or leave the area.

Washington, D.C., and the states of Virginia, Maryland, and Pennsylvania are providing millions of dollars to help reduce the amount of nutrients in the Chesapeake Bay. Much of the money goes to groups who study how excess nutrients affect the bay's ecosystem. Some of the money is spent on teaching farmers and homeowners to use less fertilizer on their crops and lawns.

All of the organizations working to save the bay encourage each person to find out how he or she can help. With everyone's participation, the Chesapeake Bay may have a better future.

Virginia's Famous People

◀ WARREN BEATTY

ACTORS

Warren Beatty (born 1937) is an actor, director, and producer from Richmond. He starred in the films *Heaven Can Wait, Reds,* and *Dick Tracy.* He is the brother of actress Shirley MacLaine.

Shirley MacLaine (born 1934) is an actress, dancer, and author. She has starred in many films, including *Terms of Endearment* and *Steel Magnolias.* The sister of actor Warren Beatty, MacLaine grew up in Richmond.

George C. Scott (born 1927) is from Wise, Virginia. One of his most famous movies is *Patton,* in which he portrays a general in World War II.

SHIRLEY ▶
MACLAINE

▲ ARTHUR ASHE

◀ GEORGE C. SCOTT

ATHLETES

Arthur Ashe (born 1943) is a former professional tennis player from Richmond. In 1975 he became the first black person to win the men's singles in tennis at Wimbledon, England.

Moses Malone (born 1955) is a basketball player who grew up in Petersburg, Virginia. A center for the Washington Bullets, Malone began his professional career in the late 1970s.

EXPLORERS

William Clark (1770–1838) was born in Caroline County, Virginia. In 1804 President Thomas Jefferson sent Clark and Meriwether Lewis to explore western territories that the United States had just purchased from France.

Meriwether Lewis (1774–1809) was born in Albemarle County, Virginia. He was a leader of the Lewis and Clark expedition. The information Lewis and Clark gathered on their two-year exploration of the West encouraged curious pioneers to settle the recently acquired U.S. territories.

INVENTORS

Thomas Jefferson (1743–1826) was born in Albemarle County, Virginia. Jefferson is best known as the author of the Declaration of Independence and as the third president of the United States. Jefferson said, "It is wonderful how much may be done if we are always doing." He took his own advice and spent his spare time designing buildings and inventing gadgets. He designed the University of Virginia, Virginia's state capitol building, and his home, Monticello. He invented the swivel chair and a clock that told not only the time but also the day of the week.

Cyrus Hall McCormick (1809–1884) invented a machine called a reaper in a workshop near his farm in Rockbridge County, Virginia. With McCormick's invention, farmers no longer had to cut grain from their fields by hand, and they could harvest the grain faster than ever before.

▲ LEWIS and CLARK

PATRIOTS & REBELS

Patrick Henry (1736–1799) was born in Hanover County, Virginia. Before the American Revolution broke out, he urged colonists to break ties with Great Britain. His most famous speech includes the words, "Give me liberty or give me death!"

Robert E. Lee (1807–1870) was born in Stratford, Virginia. Lee became the commander of the Confederate army during the Civil War. Although he fought for the South, he wished to see the United States remain one country.

Nat Turner (1800–1831) was born a slave in Southampton County, Virginia. He and his followers led a rebellion against slavery by killing 60 slave owners and freeing the laborers. He planned to free more slaves but was captured and hanged.

POLITICIANS

Harry F. Byrd, Sr. (1887–1966), helped reorganize the state government while he was governor of Virginia from 1926 to 1930. Byrd became a U.S. senator representing Virginia in 1933. He served for 30 years.

L. Douglas Wilder (born 1931) was elected governor of Virginia in 1989. Born in Richmond, Wilder is the first black person ever to be elected governor in the United States.

◀ ROBERT E. LEE

▲ NAT TURNER

◀ HARRY F. BYRD, SR.

SINGERS

Pearl Bailey (1918–1990) was born in Newport News, Virginia. She was a singer and actress best known for her starring role in the Broadway musical *Hello Dolly*.

Patsy Cline (1932–1963) was born in Winchester, Virginia. She was a country music singer whose career ended early when she died in a plane crash. Her hit singles include "Sweet Dreams."

Ella Fitzgerald (born 1918) is a jazz singer who has won eight Grammy awards. Born in Newport News, Virginia, Fitzgerald has been called the First Lady of Song.

▲ PEARL BAILEY

◀ ELLA FITZGERALD

64

William Henry Harrison (1773–1841) was born in the county of Charles City, Virginia. He became the ninth president of the United States in 1840. His famous campaign slogan, "Tippecanoe and Tyler too," came from the nickname (Tippecanoe) he earned during an Indian battle and from the last name of his running mate, John Tyler. Harrison died of pneumonia after only one month in office.

George Washington (1732–1799) was born in Westmoreland County, Virginia. He became the first president of the United States in 1789 and served in that office until 1797. Washington is called the Father of Our Country.

◀ WILLIAM HENRY HARRISON

GEORGE WASHINGTON ▶

WRITERS & EDUCATORS

Willa Cather (1873–1947) was born in Winchester, Virginia. A writer, Cather won the Pulitzer Prize for her novel *One of Ours*. Some of her other books are *O Pioneers!* and *Death Comes for the Archbishop*.

Booker T. Washington (1856–1915) was born in Franklin County, Virginia. In 1881 he founded Tuskegee University, a college in Alabama for black students. He wrote his autobiography, *Up from Slavery*, in 1901.

Tom Wolfe (born 1931) is an author from Richmond. His bestsellers include *The Electric Kool-Aid Acid Test* and *Bonfire of the Vanities*.

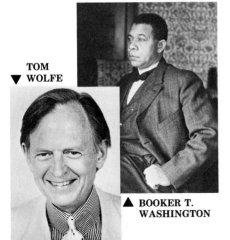

TOM ▼ WOLFE

▲ BOOKER T. WASHINGTON

65

Facts-at-a-Glance

Nickname: Old Dominion
Song: "Carry Me Back to Old Virginia"
Motto: *Sic Semper Tyrannis*
  (Thus Always to Tyrants)
Flower: flowering dogwood
Tree: flowering dogwood
Bird: cardinal

Population: 6,157,000 (1990 estimate)
Rank in population, nationwide: 12th
Area: 40,767 sq mi (105,586 sq km)
Rank in area, nationwide: 36th
Date and ranking of statehood:
  June 25, 1788, the 10th state
Capital: Richmond
Major cities (and populations*):
  Virginia Beach (333,400), Norfolk (274,800),
  Richmond (217,700), Newport News (161,700),
  Hampton (126,000)
U.S. senators: 2
U.S. representatives: 10
Electoral votes: 12

*1986 estimates

Places to visit: Arlington National Cemetery in Arlington, Luray Caverns in Shenandoah National Park, Mount Vernon near Alexandria, Virginia Beach, Williamsburg

Annual events: Dogwood Festival in Charlottesville (April), Re-enactment of the Battle of New Market in New Market (May), Harborfest in Norfolk (June), Chincoteague Annual Pony Swim and Auction (July), Neptune Festival in Virginia Beach (Sept.)

Average January temperature: 36°F (2°C)   **Average July temperature:** 75°F (24°C)

Natural resources: soil, coal, marble, limestone, clay, natural gas, petroleum, gemstones

Agricultural products: beef cattle, milk, chickens, tobacco, corn, hay, soybeans

Manufactured goods: tobacco products, chemicals, food products, electrical machinery and equipment, printed materials, textiles, paper products, rubber and plastics products

ENDANGERED SPECIES
Mammals—northern flying squirrel, Virginia big-eared bat, water shrew
Birds—bald eagle, loggerhead shrike, piping plover
Reptiles—bog turtle, chicken turtle, leatherback sea turtle
Fish—blackbanded sunfish, spotfin chub, tippecanoe darter
Plants—long-stalked holly, piratebush, round leaf birch, swamp-pink, Virginia sneezeweed

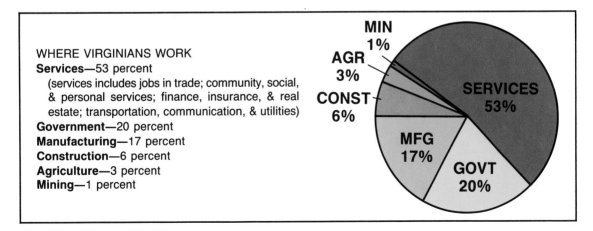

WHERE VIRGINIANS WORK
Services—53 percent
  (services includes jobs in trade; community, social, & personal services; finance, insurance, & real estate; transportation, communication, & utilities)
Government—20 percent
Manufacturing—17 percent
Construction—6 percent
Agriculture—3 percent
Mining—1 percent

MIN
1%
AGR
3%
CONST
6%
SERVICES
53%
MFG
17%
GOVT
20%

Glossary

bay A part of a sea or lake that cuts into a coastline, forming a curve; an inlet.

civil rights The rights of all citizens—regardless of race, religion, sex—to enjoy life, liberty, property, and equal protection under the law.

colony A territory ruled by a country some distance away.

constitution The system of basic laws or rules of a government, society, or organization. The document in which these laws or rules are written.

governor The person elected to be head of a state in the United States.

immigrant A person who moves into a foreign country and settles there.

lagoon A shallow lake or pond, especially one that joins a larger body of water.

marsh A spongy wetland soaked with water for long periods of time. Marshes are usually treeless; grasses are the main form of vegetation.

nutrient runoff Water from rain or melted snow that flows over land and carries nutrients from the ground to streams, lakes, oceans, and other bodies of water.

peninsula A stretch of land almost completely surrounded by water.

plantation A large estate, usually in a warm climate, on which crops are grown by workers who live on the estate. In the past, plantation owners often used slave labor.

Reconstruction The period from 1865 to 1877 during which the U.S. government brought the Southern states back into the Union after the Civil War. Before rejoining the Union, the Southern states had to pass laws allowing black men to vote. Places destroyed in the war were rebuilt and industries were developed.

swamp A wetland permanently soaked with water. Woody plants (trees and shrubs) are the main form of vegetation.

Index